"Whoever does not visit Paris regularly will never really be elegant."

Balzac, 1815

PARIS
FLEA MARKET

HERBERT
YPMA

PHOTOGRAPHS BY
RENÉ AND BARBARA STOELTIE

STEWART, TABORI & CHANG
NEW YORK

PAGES 2–3

'A French room begins with the fireplace,' says antiquarian André de Cacqueray. Fireplace surrounds in Parisian homes are traditionally deeper than those in London because they were designed to hold an impressive artifact such as a bust or a family heirloom. In line with tradition but not bound by it, Florence Dostal uses her Louis XV mantelpiece to display her Tin Tin busts, found at a local flea market, against walls painted Prussian blue.

PAGES 4–5

After dark the only sources of light even in the most splendid 18th-century Paris interiors were candles and the fireplace. Ledgers and accounts for interior decoration at the time show that far more money was spent proportionately on candlesticks than on any other aspect of an interior's decoration. An entire apartment could be panelled and furnished for the price of one pair of candlesticks or a fancy candelabra. Little wonder

then that there is still such a wide choice of these 18th-century 'utilities' available today.

PAGES 6–7

Until the Napoleonic Wars, no education was considered complete without the Grand Tour, which often included a visit to the ancient ruins of the Roman Empire. And no tour was complete without the ubiquitous busts, urns, statues and drawings that returned as architectural souvenirs. This was the start of a tradition in French interior decoration that is still going strong. Irrespective of style, taste and preferences, no self-respecting Parisian's home is complete without some sculpted reference to antiquity.

PAGE 8

The French are, perhaps more than any other nation, 'indefatigable foragers'. A detail from the completely eclectic but beautiful collection of **objets** in the apartment of Gilles Dufour, Karl Lagerfeld's assistant, is a fine example. There are no

rules. His home is like a shell – a setting for one's memories and discoveries. Pink paper, casually bunched around a Sèvres porcelain lamp base, a bâteau of crystal beads and a layer of fabric textures and patterns follow nothing but the inhabitant's moods and impulses.

PAGE 12

Toile de Jouy (meaning simply 'cloth from Jouy'), printed with scenes of everyday French life, is still covetously collected almost 230 years after its origins in the little village of Jouy, close to Versailles. Made by an incredibly complex process which was developed by Christophe-Philippe Oberkampf, these rose madder cottons were a source of tremendous pride to the Emperor Napoleon who was dedicated to nurturing and supporting French industry and craft. Upon meeting Oberkampf, Napoleon exclaimed that they were both, in their own ways, fighting the good fight against the English, but that he (Oberkampf) appeared to be the more successful.

To my parents, Carla and Peter, who have given me a more interesting and adventurous life than anyone could possibly hope for.

First published in Great Britain in 1996 by Thames and Hudson Ltd, London

Published in 1996 and distributed in the U.S. by
Stewart, Tabori & Chang,
a division of U.S. Media Holdings, Inc.
575 Broadway, New York, NY 10012

Distributed in Canada by General Publishing Co. Ltd.,
30 Lesmill Road, Don Mills, Ontario, Canada M3B 2T6

Library of Congress Catalog Card Number: 96-68725
ISBN: 1-55670-500-X

Printed in Singapore
10 9 8 7 6 5 4 3 2 1

CONTENTS

INTRODUCTION

Paris. A city of great art and dazzling architecture. How many books and poems and songs have been dedicated to this city of romance and glamour … The centre of its nation's life, Paris is admired, envied and imitated by half the world.

And always the style of Paris has been crucial to this hive of intellectual and artistic activity. As David McFadden writes in *L'Art de Vivre*: 'In France, the "arts" of living cannot be separated from "the art of living".'

From an extraordinary heritage of finery in the decorative arts, a veritable legend of man-made beauty, Parisians have absorbed an acute awareness and appreciation of the beauty of *objets* and the manner in which they can enrich one's life. This is at the very core of what can be described as French taste. A frequent American visitor to Paris once explained it in remarkably lucid terms: 'This is an urban French sensibility. Beautiful apartments in Paris are rarely "decorated": there are simply objects and pieces of furniture that someone loves, treated like works of art.'

The objects she refers to are *objets trouvés*, the personal treasures that can can be found in the atelier of a celebrated or an unknown *artiste*, at the famous *marchés aux puces* (the Paris flea markets), in the window of an expensive Left Bank *antiquaire*, on one of the massive merchandise floors of a *grand magasin* or lying abandoned in a cobbled alley or on a busy streetcorner. The rule, as quoted by the flamboyant Duc de Choiseul more than two centuries ago, is 'there are no rules'. Everything goes, as long as it is freewheeling, nostalgic and ephemeral – and all to excess!

If indeed the home is a shell – 'a setting for one's memories and discoveries, the place one comes back to when one finds them' – then Paris must be the most beautiful of all shells.

1

INTERIORS

We are a curious race. We value our privacy, yet given half a chance we are more than prepared to take a good look around our neighbour's house. How people live creates in us an almost intuitive and insatiable curiosity.

CHIC

COMIC

At first glance, this is not your typical Parisian abode. Yet in character this house, a converted artist's studio in the famous quarters of Montparnasse, reveals a streak that is quintessentially French: an abiding fascination with the *folie*.

The history of the French decorative arts returns again and again to the absurd and the extreme. These are the best remembered and the most fondly recalled of French history: how the Comte d'Artois won a bet with Marie Antoinette by completing his *folie de bagatelle* in under 64 days; how Louis XVI, concerned for Marie Antoinette's melancholy yearning, built her a neo-classical fantasy complete with grotto, where imaginary cows would yield imaginary milk; how Beistegui famously commissioned a minimalist temple from Le Corbusier and then filled it with 'baroque monstrosities', including fake grass and a Louis XV fireplace surround outside on the roof. Jean-Michel Frank, 1930s guru of monochromatic chic, was best known and admired for his office, a smallish space that in a self-parodying way 'distorted' typical 18th-century panelling to look like something out of a Tom and Jerry cartoon, the only decoration being a Diego Giacometti plaster hand holding up a blackboard on which thoughts for the day would be written.

The love of *folie* runs in an unbroken tradition. But there are some rules to this game. First and foremost is that there is absolutely no merit whatsoever in 'trying to be different'. The charm of a true *folie* is that the creator sees absolutely nothing out of the ordinary about it. It must simply be a visual manifestation of their individuality. Florence Dostal gets full marks. She is certainly not cut from the average cloth and she has created her home purely in response to her own inner voice.

Like most genuine follies Dostal's comes with its own charming fairy tale. As a little girl Florence would walk past these studios on her way to school and she would promise herself that one day she would live in one of them. In the interim she developed a certain artistic eye which, rather than to canvas, she applied to socks. And only socks. The French, as she twigged, have a thing about socks. Mitterrand was not exactly a 'dandy' when it came to dressing but he would often be photographed with a pair of bright pink socks under a rather drab beige suit. Dostal's company does nothing but bright socks. Her brand, Achille, is a genuine business success story and, true to her own promise, she finally purchased her own dream home.

The tall building in the shadow of the Tour Montparnasse, which at one time housed a roll-call of famous artists including Man Ray and the exotic Kiki de Montparnasse, was hardly an architectural *tour de force*. It still had an old wooden ladder staircase and a suspect and dreary mezzanine, but it had good bones. With the help of her friend and architect François Jantzen, she set about turning it into what design author Barbara Stoeltie describes as 'a visual poke in the eye' – no polite faded tones or discreet little pieces of furniture for Dostal. Apart from the colours, lilac pink for the living areas, Prussian blue for the bedroom and lollipop pink for the dressing room, the most imposing new feature was the curvilinear staircase – a spectacular piece of moulded reinforced concrete straight out of the Folies Bergère. But Dostal's fantasy did not end with a colour candybox and a *Gone with the Wind* staircase.

Stucco craftsmen from Auberlet and Laurent were brought in to make plaster *passementerie* and matching knots to decorate the walls: like the icing on a cake, only on a monumental scale. An oversize couch was made to Dostal's design following her recollection of one she had seen in a Mickey Mouse cartoon, crazy Ingo Maurer-designed lights, essentially naked bulbs with wings, adorn the ceiling like extravagant moths and flea market finds such as an original piece of 1950s kitchen furniture were transformed with more coats of a popsicle-green-coloured paint. Marsupial, Fred and Barney Flintstone, Donald Duck and other cartoon characters take up strategic places of importance in Dostal's overall scheme – all of which goes to prove that there is, as with all self-respecting creators of a *folie*, method in her madness.

PREVIOUS PAGE (16)
Painted an 'almost unbearable' tone of lilac, Florence Dostal's artist's atelier in Montparnasse is the signature of a person who is not afraid to follow her personal preferences. In a light-filled corner by the large expanses of glass, she has created a still life with a small bust and statuette, a reminder of the Parisian taste for sculpture.

PREVIOUS PAGES (18–19)
An 'impossibly dreary' wooden staircase was replaced by a spectacular reinforced concrete

staircase and a wrought-iron banister executed in a style inspired by the work of famous 1940s designer Gilbert Poillerat. Her taste in furniture, perhaps best descibed as offbeat, obscure and original, disguises a careful and inspired choice of pedigree pieces by the more intellectual of contemporary designers. An 'Ellipse' commode by American designers Godley and Schwann is combined with 'Mary Poppins' lights by Tom Tilleul, a 'molten footstool' by Surrealist Gaetano Pesce and an excessively baroque armchair.

OPPOSITE
The kitchen is a strong continuation of Dostal's cleverly original approach. Candy-coloured 'Series 7' chairs designed by Arne Jacobsen are combined with a Venetian chandelier custom-made in Murano, which in turn is juxtaposed with the 1950s streamline aesthetic of the 'fly' kitchen units by Feretti and the 'aeroplane wing' aesthetic of the lamp by Tom Tilleul … diverse pieces, brought together rather successfully by the common ingredients of curvaceous shape and allegorical wit.

A

COOL

EXACTITUDE

'A cool exactitude' is how author Klaus Jurgen Sembach describes the style of the 1930s. Elegant contours, subdued colours and sensitivity to materials were the hallmarks of the style of this period and 'elegance' and 'cosmopolitanism' were the key words. Precision marked every detail and the 'cool assurance' with which beautiful and costly materials were used to embellish surfaces heightened the spell even further. Even fashion followed the same path as architecture and interiors. 'Clothes around 1930 were, like the architecture, both functional and sensuous, combining a sporting, casual look with a sense of refinement and inevitability. All unnecessary details were avoided, yet opportunities for unobtrusive luxury remained.' Sembach goes so far as to suggest that 'the style of 1930s is essentially the style of the twentieth century as a whole'.

It is difficult to disagree. The architecture of Mies van der Rohe and Le Corbusier, the photography of Cartier Bresson, Beaton, Hoyningen Heune and Man Ray, the graphic design of Cassandre, the interiors of Eileen Gray and Jean-Michel Frank and the fashion of Coco Chanel and Elsa Schiaparelli formed the foundations of the visual world that we are used to today. An astonishing formal unity prevailed in all disciplines, which resulted in the creation of perhaps the clearest guidelines for how to live in the modern world.

It was a style of lucidity and maturity. And it is no coincidence that the style of the 1930s finds resonance today in the work of designer Frédéric Méchiche; for Méchiche, along with many other Parisian designers, takes the influence of the 1930s very seriously indeed.

It was an era of *chic* and glamour and romance, when Paris was once again at the very centre of this *beau monde*, particularly in terms of creating spectacular settings.

'Interior decorating', according to *Vogue* in January 1935, had become 'the smartest of all professions'. Le Corbusier and Pierre Jeanneret designed 'a very modern' apartment for the eccentric aristocrat Charles de Beistegui, with an 'astonishing suspended staircase' painted pale blue and white and with a crystal handrail; Cole Porter tinkered away in his Paris apartment surrounded by Jean-Michel Frank's straw marquetry creations on polished parquet floors bedecked with zebra-skin rugs; Dr Jean Dalsace commissioned the famous Maison de Verre (House of Glass) from architect Pierre Chareau; and Vicomte Charles de Noailles's Paris apartment, covered in tiles of glazed parchment by Jean-Michel Frank, became one of the most widely published and acclaimed interiors.

It was an era rich in sources of inspiration.

In the lacquer screens by Eileen Gray, the opulently sculptural furniture designed by Jules Leleu and the beautifully restrained monochromatic interiors of Frank, it is possible to detect an 'elitism' – 'a degree of perfection' which Sembach describes as 'almost merciless'.

And it is perhaps this trait – a merciless perfectionism – that establishes the most immediate link between Méchiche's work and the style of the 1930s. Detractors say he will go to almost any length to impose his own style, 'to keep churning out chalky walls, striped fabrics and dinky chandeliers', but in reality his work is far more urbane, and far more French, than first impressions might suggest. His real signature stems from a sophisticated mix of *objets* from different periods and styles fastidiously brought together by an intelligent and well-informed eye.

He shares with Napoleon a preference for striped fabrics and in furniture he leans towards the masters of the French 18th century, combined with a taste for African masks (a preference that has its roots in the 1930s when the arts of tribal Africa were widely displayed, appreciated and collected in Paris), the odd mythology-inspired Cocteau drawing, a scattering of contemporary design pieces and a not insignificant *assemblage* of 20th-century art. These *objets*, the real components of his style, are all so carefully and meticulously selected that they, like the style of the 1930s, have a real unity of quality. 'I am invariably first attracted to quality in an object or piece of furniture,' says Méchiche. 'I try to tell my clients that you should avoid admiring the artistic output of a given epoch if at the same time you are not prepared to judge the sincerity of its creators by the most stringent standards.'

The most stringent standards of all are applied to his own home, photographed here, where Méchiche is free to sort history's 'major' talents from its 'minor' ones.

PREVIOUS PAGE (22)
The space underneath a graceful staircase was used by Méchiche for his library of art and design books. In the foreground an urn on top of a plain plinth is typical of the ubiquitous Parisian taste for antiquity. A sofa designed by Méchiche, upholstered in a deep blue sateen silk (which borders on being purple) adds a dash of regal colour to an interior that is otherwise all light and air.

OPPOSITE PAGE
Frédéric Méchiche's new home is an elegant duplex in the Marais, the original quarter for Paris's aristocrats which is now making a comeback as a fashionable place to live. The interior is a testament to his personal decorative preferences, such as these Louis XVI chairs, upholstered in his signature striped fabric, casually arranged, somewhat in the manner of the 18th century when a dining room was any room where chairs were placed around a table.

1	2	3	4
5	6	7	8

1

A Restoration lyre back chair, a spirally carved timber rod and a Miro painting constitute a still life in Méchiche's previous abode, a large converted warehouse near the Bastille. He has since moved, but the composition is typical and timeless.

2

The mounted remnant of an Egyptian funerary mask sits on a Louis XV fireplace amidst Frédéric's collection of art books. The taste for Egyptian artifacts dates back to the time of Napoleon's military campaign and has endured ever since.

3

One of the most distinctive elements of his design is the tension between the orderly and the disordered. In an interior of superb panelling and crystal chandeliers, framed images of all kinds are arranged haphazardly.

4

A pair of Louis XVI pink upholstered chairs combined with tribal sculpture on a metal garden table and a Miro painting in an old frame attest to Frédéric Méchiche's great talent for combining disparate objects of beauty.

5

Méchiche's fondness for 18th-century chairs is combined here with a Moroccan tea table. He avoids the jewel casket type of room stuffed with works of art. Instead, contrast between epochs and styles provide a creative tension.

6

*Despite his unerring eye for **objets** of great beauty, Méchiche is still capable of slipping a dog-eared postcard next to a priceless painting. It is this love of the unexpected, the respect for the deliberate mistake, that is so Parisian.*

7

Napoleon was very fond of striped fabric and used it extensively for the decoration of all of his state and private homes. Stripes are also such a favourite with Méchiche that they are almost a trademark for his work.

8

A terracotta urn perched on a classically inspired plinth made from packing crate timber: a taste for antiquity has been the single most enduring characteristic of the French decorative arts over the past three centuries.

O

PPOSITE PAGE

The bathroom in his new duplex is a departure from his usual white interiors. Taking his cue from the building's historical pedigree, a zinc bath, Louis XVI chairs and a Directoire zinc cistern are set off by the tiled floor.

THE
LOVE
OF
LUXE

'Eighteenth-century Hollywood' is how author Barbara Stoeltie describes the style of the interior created by Frédéric Méchiche for French pop star Karen Cheryl – a place that combines the *luxe* and grandeur of 18th-century France with the glamour of Hollywood.

Grandeur, glamour, luxury: these are the qualities so admired by the French: the result of an undeniably impressive historical legacy. The decadent opulence of the Bourbon court is, of course, legendary: the Sun King and his Versailles were perhaps the historical ultimate in grandeur. But the Revolution was meant to change all that. No more extravagance; equality was the catchword. Yet, only a few years later, Napoleon was at it in his own grand way. In fact, his architects used to joke that he could not conceive of anything being important if it was not 'monumental'. He had a taste for luxury, for exquisite objects and furnishings, and it is a historical fact that the famous French luxury industries were set in motion by Napoleon's patronage. Fuelled by the demand of the newly emerging middle classes, French goods from porcelain to glass took their place as second to none. Names such as Christofle (established 1830), Puiforcat (1820) and Hermès (1837), building on reputations that were already well established over a century ago, have become almost generic for the materials in which they work. Baccarat, for example, is automatically associated with crystal, as Christofle is with silver tableware.

By the time of Napoleon III, France was the leader in the world of the decorative arts, and more than ever the possession of beautiful objects was a sign of affluence. A curious, ironic and completely French preference evolved in terms of these items of desire. Handcrafted, one-of-a-kind *objets* were esteemed, even when they were provided by the manufacturing sector. Because of this distinction, design and the decorative arts in France have continued to reveal the same profile to the present day: neither 'studio craft' nor 'industrial design' has ever held the same kind of appeal as the handmade *objets* produced in multiples.

Socially, the norm developed in the late 1800s for setting the boundaries of acceptable and unacceptable 'excess' has changed little up to the present day. It was not considered *de bon ton*, for instance, to spend lavishly as the aristocracy used to, but 'comfortable opulence' was desirable and even morally condoned. It was conveniently agreed that 'a strong family feeling flourishes in a warm and luxurious interior'. This, of course, was nothing more than a cleverly conceived smokescreen: the French taste for luxury has never been surrendered, just disguised.

Disguise is an appropriate metaphor for Méchiche's conversion of what was once a rather banal 1940s house. 'I love 1940s American films,' he explains, 'where you get those interiors with vast sofas and out-of-proportion lamps – things that look incredibly *chic* to start with but turn out to be rather less so on closer inspection and keep you perpetually on tenterhooks in case the camera should accidentally reveal that there's no ceiling.'

This 'tension' was a key ingredient in creating the interior. It was also rather a blessing that the owner, a coquettish, independent-minded pop star described by Barbara Stoeltie as 'a romantic figure out of a novel by Colette', arrived empty-handed. She did not own a thing. It allowed Méchiche to start from absolute scratch – as on a film set.

Cheryl did, however, bring a strong set of priorities to the task. 'I regard my private life as sacrosanct,' she would say, 'and if I decide to buy myself a dream, I'll have that dream tailor-made.' Méchiche's tailoring included just about everything in sight: the bleached parquet floor, the chalky fireplace with the hearth full of white sprayed logs, the alcoves adorned with plaster drapery and some softly undulating 'romantic' sofas that seem to fit her like a glove. But not all is *faux*. Two Louis XVI medallion chairs, a pair of enigmatic oil portraits and a hefty painting over the fireplace attest to the fact that virtually no truly French interior is complete without the essential touch of *l'école française dix-huitième*.

PREVIOUS PAGE (30)
An 18th-century Venetian console, a reproduction Roman lamp and a typically French 18th-century medallion portrait look perfectly at home against the 'faux' 18th-century panelling painted on the walls of what was originally an undistinguished 1940s house. Pop star Karen Cheryl describes her house as a blend of Mae West and the **école française dix-huitième**: a stage-set home for a professional performer.*

OPPOSITE PAGE
Designer and interior architect Frédéric Méchiche created the ambience that his client Karen Cheryl wanted from what were just 'bare bones'. He designed the curvaceous 1940s-inspired furniture and the impressively scaled fireplace, the plaster-dipped curtains around the windows and mirrors and the soft effect of the clotted-cream-coloured trompe-l'oeil panelling. Classical touches are reinforced here and there by the Louis XVI medallion chairs and the fake Roman pedestal tables.*

A
TASTE
FOR
ANTIQUITY

The style of the period immediately following the Revolution was known as *'le goût grec'*, when the swinging pendulum of taste in fashion, architecture and interiors settled on the classicism of ancient Greece and Rome – in truth, a romanticized version of the classics, drawn from antiquity with more fantasy than accuracy.

A style that came from studying Roman arches, Greek vases and Etruscan tombs, *le goût grec* was hardly precise in academic terms but it suited the times. To Revolutionaries smitten with ideas of social equality and ideological purity, decorative motifs borrowed from the Roman republic seemed appropriate. Neo-classicism, with its simple and strict lines, its sober greys and delicately hued monotones, stood in total contrast to the earlier *rocaille* style, so reminiscent of the fallen aristocracy.

It was not really a break in style (although it was certainly touted as such) so much as a continuation of neo-classical traits that had appeared during the reign of Louis XVI. *Le style à l'antique*, as it was also known, had a sweeping influence on post-Revolutionary Paris life. The Revolution not only granted women the right to divorce, it also liberated their bodies. Parisian women discarded their tight, heavy clothing and dressed in very low-cut, high-waisted white muslin dresses taken straight from the illustrations and paintings unearthed in the newly discovered ruins of Pompeii and Herculaneum. These daring young things, known as *les Merveilleuses*, and their male consorts, *les Incroyables*, were survivors of the countless coups, countercoups and bloody power struggles after the fall of the Bastille in 1789. They had seen enough mayhem and now had a tremendous hunger for pleasure and luxury. For the first time in French history, 'society' life was available to others beyond the aristocracy. Anyone with money could participate: bankers, traders, merchants and manufacturers became the new clients of the legions of craftsmen who had previously worked for the aristocracy. France was busy building a *république bourgeoise*, and this bourgeoisie, the new elite, had a taste for antiquity.

Urns, busts, statuettes and reliefs in marble, bronze, terracotta and biscuit were much in demand as the quintessential *objets d'art*, creating a decorative preference

A

RESPECT

FOR

AUTHENTICITY

Not all dynasties were trampled on and buried during the Revolution. Somehow, amidst the chaos and confusion, many people who had established legendary reputations under the patronage of the Bourbons managed to carry on. Some, like the esteemed Monsieur Georges Jacob, went on to even bigger and better things.

Born in 1739, Georges Jacob became *Maître Menuisier* in 1765 and made furniture for Louis XVI, including a famous pair of chairs for Marie Antoinette's *folie*, the Laiterie at Château Rambouillet. Although, like countless others, he lost substantial sums of money as a result of the Revolution, not to mention the unfortunate beheading of most of his clientele, he managed to ally himself with new names. The architects Percier and Fontaine, who went on to become Napoleon's favourites, were among his supporters, and with such connections Jacob's success with the new government was assured. The Revolution also, in a sense, liberated his talents. Under the *ancien régime*, furniture-making was strictly divided into specialized guilds. There were *menuisiers*, joiners who made furniture out of solid wood, *ébénistes*, cabinet-makers who specialized in marquetry, *tabletiers*, craftsmen who made small, highly refined objects, and so on. Georges Jacob had been an extremely gifted *menuisier*, but now, because the Revolution had done away with the guilds, he was allowed to do more than just a joiner's work.

With the patronage of Napoleon, Jacob became one of the most famous and prestigious names in furniture. At its high point, Jacob-Desmalter, as it had become known after Jacob turned the business over to his sons in 1796 (though he continued to turn his hand to his craft until 1814), employed more than 330 people in 16 workshops. Under the guidance of this next generation, Jacob-Desmalter (Desmalter being the name of the family property outside Paris) grew into one of the most prolific industrial suppliers of furniture for aristocrats and the bourgeoisie.

It is lucky, then, that Georges Jacob, his son François-Honoré and in turn his son each signed their work in an individual manner, for as history would show, these were indeed pedigree pieces, furniture so beautifully made that it would serve, almost a century later, as inspiration for the pieces designed by Art Deco masters such as Ruhlmann, Dunand and Leleu.

The French take their decorative arts history very seriously and nowhere is this more evident than in the dusty, time-encrusted world of Pierre-Hervé Wallbaum. An acknowledged authority on the Empire style, Wallbaum is a decorator-designer who works at the highest levels. Both the government and high society refer to his expertise for interiors of historical significance. It is only fitting, then, that this man not only lives in a building designed by Napoleon's favourite architects Percier and Fontaine, but that it is virtually untouched or unchanged from the time it was first built.

When he first arrived in the building, Wallbaum knew little about his neighbours on the *bel étage* and even less about their abode. When one day they moved out, Wallbaum seized the opportunity and moved in. What he found was a 19th-century interior virtually untouched by modernization. Electric light and some rudimentary plumbing were about the only concessions to the 20th century. This was better than a museum. The patina of age had encrusted the rather grand apartment, giving it a tobacco-tinted appearance that the most skilled *faux*-finish artist in the world could not hope to reproduce. Wallbaum was determined to leave it this way. For a connoisseur with a superb collection of Empire pieces, including a table made by Georges Jacob and an extremely rare, Egyptian-inspired sarcophagus made by his son François-Honoré, a more perfect place is hard to imagine. It would be like asking an Elvis Presley fanatic if they would like to live in Gracelands.

Here, among the cracked walls, the torn, tainted and stained wallpaper, the threadbare carpets, the chipped paint and the peeling ceilings, Pierre-Hervé Wallbaum has surrounded himself with remarkable treasures, brought together by a tireless collector who has won an international following for the depth of his knowledge and his commitment to authenticity. He readily admits that it often takes great discipline to avoid the temptation to restore the apartment – one bucket of soapy water and a sponge and the magical spell of authenticity would be broken.

PREVIOUS PAGE (40)
The most commanding piece in the dining room is the very rare and valuable polychrome 'Egyptian mummy' by Jacob-Desmalter. Napoleon's campaigns in Egypt captured the popular imagination and studies of Egyptian culture provided a wealth of new material and inspiration for French artisans and craftsmen.

OPPOSITE PAGE
*Cracks gape through the papered walls, smoke encrusts the woodwork, water stains and exposed wiring mark the surfaces and the columns in the dining room are definitely lopsided, but the cumulative effect in terms of atmosphere is one of rarity, character and privilege. Mood and ambience are the attributes house-proud Parisians aspire to most and this **hôtel particulier** has plenty of both. Light streaming into the tobacco-tinted dining room illuminates a table setting which reflects Pierre-Hervé Wallbaum's refined eye. Crystal, gold, porcelain and **bleu de porcelaine**-coloured candles introduce just the right amount of colour, light and sense of **luxe** to create the desired effect.*

1	2	3	4
5	6	7	8

PHOTOS IN ORDER OF
APPEARANCE – PREVIOUS PAGES (44–45)

1

The grand coffered vault of the apartment's entrance reveals the building's Empire pedigree: the designers, Charles Percier and Pierre Fontaine, also created the famous Malmaison for Napoleon and Josephine.

2

There are many imperfections here: cracks in the papered walls, water stains and exposed wiring, and the columns in the dining room even appear to be leaning. Nonetheless, the overall effect remains quite spellbinding.

3

A signed Comolli portrait head dated 1803 and a bust of Napoleon's sister, Elisa, dominate the view from the drawing room to the dining room.

4

The bedroom, like the rest of the interior, houses some important decorative objects which are restrained by the everyday manner in which they used. Despite Wallbaum's love of authenticity, his priority is comfort. The bed is attributed to Bellange, and the console table behind is signed by François-Honoré Jacob.

5

Pierre-Hervé Wallbaum has a strong preference for neo-classicism and the Empire style. He is also a stickler for detail and a firm believer in authenticity. Against the backdrop of an interior virtually untouched since the 1800s, he has carefully placed his collection of historically significant, exquisite and extraordinary pieces. A console table by Jacob-Desmalter (the work of the Jacob family, favourites of Napoleon) supports a bronze effigy of Agrippina, a pair of 19th-century oil lamps, modelled on Roman originals, and an Academy study of a male nude.

6

A bust of Hector in the fireplace and a collection of unused frames divert attention (intentionally) from all the priceless antiques Wallbaum has brought together and instead make one appreciate the atmosphere of a house that could still so easily belong to an early 19th-century connoisseur.

7

An Empire table placed in a corner of the study sits under a bronze shield, cast after the original from antiquity, and holds an impressive array of classical figures, including bronzes of Silenus and Bacchus (left, 19th century), some winged and dancing figures based on originals unearthed at Pompeii and a cast of Narcissus. The rest of the study features yet more busts and objects.

8

*The grand proportions of Wallbaum's apartment are typical of the work of Percier and Fontaine, Napoleon's favourite architects. The main rooms that lead directly from one to another comprise what was known as the **appartement de parade**, the part that one would show off. Corridors and kitchens were strictly for servants.*

Opposite Page

*Pierre-Hervé Wallbaum's desk in his authentic 19th-century apartment is cluttered with the busts, candlesticks and bowls that typify turn-of-the-century neo-classical **objets d'art**.*

A

BOLD

BLUE

BLEND

The 1960s were a difficult period for France. Not only did the riots in Paris threaten to escalate into a modern-day version of the Revolution, but for the first time in recent history France lost its pre-eminence in design and the decorative arts.

The 1960s were irreverent. The past did not matter; only the new was interesting. Every convention was turned upside-down or just plain thrown out of the window. Curvaceous, organic forms replaced classical shapes and proportions, plastic took over from just about every other material, and patterns and colours were desirable only if they were either shocking or psychedelic. It was a look for which the histori-cally minded French had little sympathy.

The French were dragging their decorative feet. At the *Domus: Formes italiennes* exhibition in 1968 at Galeries Lafayette (the first Paris department store with a design studio), the need for French industry to become more competitive internationally was underlined. Mediocre design prevailed. There were, of course, exceptions, such as Olivier Mourgue, whose futuristic designs landed him a job as production assistant on Stanley Kubrick's *2001 – A Space Odyssey*, and Pierre Paulin, who designed some beautifully free-flowing and sculptural furniture, which, ironically, was being made (as it still is) by Dutch design firm Artifort. Despite the odd French maverick, how-ever, the style of the 1960s belonged to the Italians. Although the French luxury industries were still doing well, the creative edge that France had usually all but monopolized suddenly belonged to the Guccis, Puccis and Fioruccis. Italian furni-ture, Italian fashion, Italian fabrics and Italian industrial design were, for the first time since the Renaissance, leading the world. This, however, did not stop the French from eventually adding this decade to their decorative repertoire.

In an admirably democratic process, France has managed to absorb even this dis-appointing decade – in terms of their own contribution – into its collective 'taste'. Thirty years on, the French have come to appreciate the forward-looking freshness, innovation and positivity of the 1960s. Perhaps more than in any other capital city (with the possible exception of Milan), 1960s pieces, particularly furniture, are actively bought and sold at places like the St-Ouen flea markets – the true seal of approval.

"I would hate

to live surrounded

by things that all match."

Dominique Vellay

And the Parisians are sophisticated enough to know how to deal, decoratively speaking, with plastic furniture and futuristic shapes.

Didier Ludot's home is a good example. In an apartment on the Rue de Miromesnil, there is no mistaking the bold plastic and tubular steel of Italian designers Cesare Leonardi and Franca Stagi's CL9 Ribbon chair in the drawing room. Yet this is by no means a 1960s apartment.

Against a colour background that most resembles a popular early 19th-century shade known as *bleu de porcelaine*, the interior is an odd mélange of objects, including heroic Art Deco bronze busts, some Memphis pieces and a *pouffe* upholstered in a vintage Hermès silk scarf that reveals a little about Ludot's career.

Ludot has one of the most original jobs in Paris. He is an authority on and dealer in famous *haute couture*: an *antiquaire de la couture*, probably one of the world's first antiquarians of high fashion. He tracks down creations by Dior, Balenciaga, Mainbocher, Schiaparelli and Chanel, to name but a few, and then offers them for sale in his gallery in the Palais Royal. An elite clientele relish the opportunity, of course, to buy a creation by one of the late, great couturiers.

Back in his apartment Ludot might even be opening the door for a 1980s revival. Memphis, the anti-design movement started by Ettore Sottsass which briefly – and ironically – became the most fashionable design statement in the early 1980s before almost completely disappearing at the beginning of the 1990s, is seen here successfully combined with 1960s furniture and 1920s bronzes.

PREVIOUS PAGE (48)
An Art Deco bronze set against a wall painted **bleu de porcelaine** *decorates a typically Parisian radiator. Art Deco proved to be close to French taste, reviving the beloved tradition of fine furniture-making as well as beautiful design in other disciplines. A love of fine textures and forms and delicacy in the use of materials returned for the first time since the 19th century.*

PREVIOUS PAGE (50)
A Parisian has no respect for things that match and a great love for daring and the occasional mistake. A home is sup-posed to be built around the objects one cares about and as such nothing is really out of bounds. Furniture, paintings, sculpture, bowls, vases and fabrics, found, tracked down or inherited, form the only acceptable foundation of style and elegance. In Ludot's apartment, heroic Art Deco sculpture is combined with 1980s Memphis lamps and furniture, a footstool upholstered in a Hermès 'American Indian' scarf and classic 1960s Ribbon chairs, continuous bands of fibreglass supported on cantilevered tubular steel bases, by Cesare Leonardi and Franca Stagi.

OPPOSITE PAGE
The voice of tradition resounds down through the history of the French decorative arts. Art Deco furniture acknowledges its ancestry in the craftsmanship and proportions of the 18th century: the radical fashions of couturier Poiret were inspired by the **Merveilleuses** *of the Empire period and the popularity of heroic Art Deco bronzes continues a taste for the classic busts and statues that goes back to the 18th century and the era of the Grand Tour. Two identical bronze busts are posed – dramatically and effectively – facing in the same direction.*

COLOUR

CHINA

Of all the arts the French have paid particular attention to throughout history, entertaining and *gastronomie* would have to be among their most constant focuses. As a result, a veritable legion of craftspeople thrived from enterprise related to the dining table.

Even at the height of the bloodthirsty Terror of the Revolution, condemned aristocrats, faced with the grim reality of Dr Guillotin's invention, would have the best *traiteurs* in town prepare the most delicate meals. Gastronomy became a more democratic affair after the Revolution. Around the turn of the 18th century, a major change took place in the art of the table: *service à la française* (all courses laid out at once on the table) was being replaced by *service à la russe*, in which the food was brought out one course at a time on a heated plate. Less pleasing to the eye perhaps but a lot more efficient, *service à la russe* at least ensured food was served hot and opened the way for more challenging cuisine. All of a sudden tables were less burdened with food; the new space was filled by decoration in the form of ornamental sculptures and centrepieces and vases filled with flowers and, of course, candelabras.

The elaborate ceremony of dining and table-dressing thus had a substantial influence on the decorative arts in general and it could be said that this 'art of entertaining' helped to develop the tradition of *objets d'art* being used to adorn not only the table but, in due course, the entire house.

Perhaps this is why the French value their porcelain so much. Even when he was banished to St Helena in 1815, Napoleon took his Sèvres *service de quartiers généraux*, or at least the 72 dessert plates he had left, with him. He did not use them for fear of breaking them, but would only take them down from the walls to admire them.

At that time, Sèvres porcelain had a technical and artistic perfection without equal in Europe. With Baron Denon, Napoleon's expert on antiquities, and his architects Percier and Fontaine acting as aesthetic advisers, it is little wonder that Sèvres porcelain became such a legend. It was a highly desirable item, reflected in the tradition of giving entire Sèvres services to distinguished heads of state.

"All beautiful things belong to the same age."

Oscar Wilde

Such was the prestige of porcelain that in many bourgeois homes it began to take the place of silver and gold. Painting on porcelain became very important and most pieces were completely covered, leaving no white porcelain visible. Portraits, views of important cities and refined imitations of antique cameos were common subjects. Many households commissioned specially designed display cabinets or elaborate wall brackets to allow for their collections to be visible in all their colourful glory, and it was quite customary to exhibit one's best pieces on the mantelpiece. In larger dining rooms the entire service would often be artfully arranged along the walls, to be taken down only for banquets. So central were these porcelain *objets d'art* to the owners' interiors that it was common practice to base one's entire interior colour scheme on the colour of the porcelain.

Serge Hubert, a legendary figure in the Paris antiques world, lives in an apartment painted the most exquisite shade of orange – not a colour one would find on a paint chart. This is a rich exotic tone that conjures up the type of interior atmosphere Proust would write about. And there on the mantelpiece are the plates that gave rise to the scheme … in the same colour as the room.

Hubert is an institution in Paris: famous for his exceptional 'eye', he is a magpie unfettered by predilections for a particular epoch or style. His is a daring, quixotic taste which follows only the common thread of beauty. He is from the same era as the great Madame Castaing, sharing her advantage of having experienced quite a few different styles and epochs. And even at 80 years of age he is still active.

His apartment in Paris is living proof that even the most 'modern'-minded Frenchman, a man who knew both Picasso and Cocteau, will not abandon some of the fine traditions and history of the French decorative arts despite, or perhaps exactly because of, a lifelong association with the 'avant garde'.

PREVIOUS PAGE (54)
Porcelain, clocks and candle-sticks were expensive luxuries in 18th-century France. Plates were often purely decorative and these meticulously painted, painstakingly executed pieces would often dictate the scheme for the whole house. An attempt would be made to make sure that the colour of the paint on the walls and the fabric of the upholstery matched the colour of the porcelain. The walls of

antique dealer Serge Hubert's Paris apartment are painted the same shade as the plates on his mantelpiece.

PREVIOUS PAGE (56)
The mantelpiece in Serge Hub-ert's Paris flat reveals what might be called a typically Parisian taste for antiquity. The marble medallions, busts, torsos and statues of ancient Rome and Greece continue to play an important role in Parisian

interiors. A statuette is flanked by two porcelain Chinoiserie-inspired plates.

OPPOSITE PAGE
A verdigris standard candle lamp and a chair from the Directoire period and a 19th-century portrait of an **Incroyable** *reveal Hubert's reverence for fine textures and forms: characteristics that keep history active in present-day design and decoration.*

A

MATURE

MIX

Mixing the *objets* of different epochs, styles and origins is nothing new to the French: they've been doing it for the best part of three hundred years.

Madame de Pompadour had the independence of mind in the 1740s to manifest a taste for the classics at the time when the *rocaille* (the French equivalent of the Baroque) was *de rigueur*. In her quest for antiquities she even despatched her brother to the ruins of ancient Rome to bring back drawings, paintings and souvenirs to sit alongside her Louis XV furniture and her Rococo flourishes. Marie Antoinette also fostered a taste for neo-classicism that was, in fact, to have a significant influence on the style of Louis XVI. For her Laiterie in the gardens of the Château Rambouillet, she commissioned chairs from the famous craftsman Georges Jacob that were modelled on actual furniture excavated from the ruins of Herculaneum.

This borrowing of ideas from ancient civilization was already familiar to the French court. Jean-Baptiste Colbert, Louis XIV's minister, instituted a remarkable education system that included the founding of the Académie de France in Rome and a competition that had an extraordinary impact on the arts in France, the Grand Prix de Rome. More exotically, the trend-setting Comte d'Artois, the future Charles X, started a new fashion in 1777 called *le goût turc*, which, with its *faux*-Oriental splendour, was found particularly apt for boudoirs – though not for the entire house.

Even at the time of Napoleon, despite the uniform rigour of the Emperor's style, the publication of Baron Denon's wildly successful book, *Voyage dans la Basse et la Haute Egypte*, launched an unprecedented demand for Egyptian obelisks, pyramids and sphinxes, encrusted, sculpted or painted on everything from desks to plates.

By the late 19th century, eclecticism was the rule, not the exception. Gothic, Renaissance, Empire, Directoire, Louis XIV, XV and XVI, as well as Chinoiserie and Japonisme, represented just some of the decorative styles that one could explore in creating an interior and the 'opulent extreme' of using all of them at once became known as *le goût Rothschild*. The 20th century has added even more styles to the list: Art Deco, a taste for African *objets d'art*, the minimal, angular approach of the 'modern movement' and, finally, the colourful abandon of the 1960s.

Even in France, where the notion of *le mix* is well established, an individual has to be very secure in his or her own tastes to choose between all these styles. Not that it is impossible. As Oscar Wilde wrote: 'All objects of beauty belong to the same age'.

With great daring, flair and humour, Rémy le Fur has managed to combine, in one typically grand Parisian apartment, furniture, art and *objets* from just about every decorative epoch. African masks, 1950s furniture, classical busts, Art Deco reliefs, modern art, 1960s rugs, neo-classical tables, a 1930s commode, Louis XV fireplaces, Empire tiled floors, Pop Art, Directoire chairs – a comprehensive historical *mise en scène* set against the high ceilings, tall slender windows and panelled rooms of a 19th-century Parisian apartment.

Despite the extraordinary diversity and historical range of its contents, the apartment does not, however, project the stuffy, 'don't touch' atmosphere of a museum, nor does it strain under the cumulative effect of all these styles and periods. It projects the feeling of a shell that haphazardly holds together all the bits and pieces that the owner has stumbled across in a lifetime. That this interior hasn't the slightest hint of pomp or pretension makes it a decorative *tour de force*.

Admittedly, Rémy le Fur has had a lot of practice. As one of France's most renowned auctioneers (Poulain & Le Fur) he spends most of his working life using his highly trained eye. From classic cars to precious antiques and modern art, he discerns objects of beauty for a living – experience he has used in creating this extraordinarily eclectic interior and proving, in the process, that Mr Wilde was a wise old sage indeed.

PREVIOUS PAGE (60)

*'An innovative mélange that ensures a simple yet sophisticated atmosphere' is an apt description of Rémy le Fur's apartment. 'How French!' is another. All the hallmarks are here: a taste for antiquity, modern furniture, a few African pieces and some serious contemporary art. A completely oversize bust of Juno – the same as the one in Goethe's house in Weimar, based on the original in Rome – guards over an **eau de Nile**-painted room. The chair in the foreground is made from a 'No overtaking' traffic sign.*

PREVIOUS PAGES (62–63)

Le Fur believes that style clashes can be exciting and this room just about proves it. Bordering on bad taste, a great compliment in cosmopolitan Paris, a check-pattern marble tiled floor, typical of early Empire interiors, combines with a neo-classical coffee table and a vivid yellow modern painting. Purple silk (very Roman) swathes windows and chair.

OPPOSITE PAGE

In a room dominated by a carpet designed by Le Fur himself, a Louis XV fireplace

sits alongside African art and a plaster relief from the 1920s.

FOLLOWING PAGES (66–67)

Le Fur gets his inspiration from many sources. An American Indian headdress is as appropriate to his panelled apartment as a classical frieze, and a Charles Eames moulded plywood lounge chair shoulders a commode originally made by Jantzen for the Duchess of Windsor. Renaissance man had a great curiosity for different cultures. Le Fur's daring mix, then, is really a continuation of a gentleman's tradition.

THE
EMULATION
OF
EMPIRE

Empire was a style largely influenced by the personality of one man – Napoleon Bonaparte. When this daringly successful military prodigy, the star graduate of the academy in Paris and the country's youngest ever general, boldly declared himself Emperor, he took over the leadership of a country that was a shadow of its former self.

With France torn apart by civil war, from the destruction of the aristocracy to the disbanding of the formerly quite *solidaire* craft guilds, Napoleon set about the mammoth task of rebuilding the state and the economy.

Napoleon's relatively short reign (ten years) was a period of extraordinary development for the arts and crafts in France. Just as he knew how to surround himself with the best military advisers, he also managed to take into his employ the best artists in Europe. The economic importance of the decorative arts to the general health and well-being of France was perceived by Napoleon. The Empire provided massive assistance to workshops, encouraged technical innovation, funded elaborate schooling and served as one of the biggest-spending clients of these various artisan industries. Napoleon reorganized the floundering Sèvres porcelain factory to create a *manufacture impériale*, he patronized the silk weavers of Lyon, he began massive refurbishment of various important houses destroyed by the Revolution, providing ample work for France's gifted furniture-makers; and in his zealous promotion of these arts, it could be said that he founded the luxury industries, many of which are still going today, such as Puiforcat, Christofle, Baccarat and Hermès.

Le Style Empire was thus a style that answered the newly emerging middle classes' desire for luxury, a new market which the manufacturers of luxury goods were particularly good at exploiting. This delighted Napoleon, since emulation of the Emperor (and his style) was encouraged amongst the bourgeoisie. Ever the strategist, Napoleon had created a society in which to be stylish was also to be patriotic.

It was a remarkable age, both heroic and tragic. The collapse of the Empire in 1815 ended an epic chapter in the country's history. But the lessons of Napoleon's style – proportion, order and harmony, and attention to detail and finish – were not forgotten. Their influence in French design can still be seen today.

Roberto Bergero's Parisian apartment is a prime example. Painted throughout in a neo-classical colour popularly referred to as 'Naples yellow' (which was also quite a favourite with Napoleon), the space is, with the exception of a Venetian mirror, furnished in the Empire style. Not unlike the Stoelties and their apartment (pages 34–39), his fondness for Empire seems to be a direct result of living in Paris. The traditions and rich decorative history of this provocative city have, like a cult religion, captured another convert. Born in Argentina, Bergero thinks of himself more as an Italian: he was brought up in an Argentinian community dominated by Italian immigrants, so it is the language he grew up with. Since then he has been many things in many places. He is a stylist, a decorator, a designer…an artist. Bergero came to Paris from Sweden, where he had been employed by Ikea. In photos of his previous apartment, which have been published extensively, traces of his Swedish experience can still be seen in the odd, albeit heavily disguised, Ikea occasional tables.

In his new apartment, however, he has succumbed to the legacy of Napoleon's style. Whereas his previous home might best have been described as 'colourfully eclectic', his new abode is strictly neo-classical. Gone are the 'busy' bits and pieces painted in many colours and patterns; in their place one finds the discipline, the harmony and the order of neo-classicism…the marble, mahogany, gilded woods, bronze and silks and spectacular beds that constitute the elements of the Empire style.

"In France, the 'arts' of living cannot be separated from 'the art of living'."

David McFadden

PREVIOUS PAGE (68)
Reflected in a Venetian mirror, Apollo is illuminated on a pediment in the window of Roberto Bergero's newly acquired apartment. It is painted entirely in a shade known as Naples yellow, a colour which became quite popular in the late 18th century after the discovery of the ruins at Pompeii and Herculaneum.

OPPOSITE
Beneath a Venetian glass mirror, a collection of Directoire and Louis XVI medallion chairs and an Empire daybed reinforce Bergero's refined neo-classical interior. The interior is arranged very much in the manner of the late 18th and early 19th centuries, when most pieces would stand against the wall and chairs would be arranged when required.

FOLLOWING PAGE (72)
Another Empire daybed, this time in mahogany, dominates one side of the main drawing room, flanked by a pair of custom-designed book etagères, a pair of Napoleonic stools and a pair of Bergero-designed black 'biscuit' urns. Ironically, despite the fact that Empire was very much a reflection of Napoleon's personal tastes, the trend towards the use of mahogany was instigated by the popularity of English Chippendale pieces, a fact that would not have pleased the Emperor, who was known to be extremely covetous and proud of the French pre-eminence in furniture- and cabinet-making.

"The appeal of the classical is that it is based on architecture and they present a sense of order, and order is what most examples of modern living most need."

Melanie Fleischmann

ART

PAUVRE

If only Louis XVI had thought of it! The notion of *art pauvre* might have saved more than just his crown. At the time, however, it was unthinkable that anyone would aspire to own anything that wasn't grand and *luxe*; only *objets* beautifully made by gifted and highly skilled craftsmen were worth possessing. In fact, it wasn't really until the advent of American artist Man Ray in the early 20th century and his peculiar (at least at the time) notion of beauty that the French would consider anything other than precious 'craftsmanship' as having any value, aesthetic or otherwise.

Man Ray did, however, have one thing in common with the French in that he was an 'indefatigable forager'. But that is where the similarity ended. He was happy with an old mattress spring, an empty matchbox or a discarded shoe sole. Because he was a bum and a hobo? Hardly. Rather, because he was an artist gifted enough to recognize, as he put it, 'the beauty in the everyday objects that surround us'. He firmly believed that the emphasis on 'technical skill' could and often did camouflage true beauty. People were being dazzled by the 'sizzle', not the 'meat'. This was a line of thinking already largely accepted in the art world at the time. To judge a painter by his 'technical proficiency' was, of course, ludicrous, yet this system of appraisal still dominated the world of the French decorative arts. After all, an entire industry had been built on the strength of French craftsmanship and it was not something they were about to give up without a jolly good fight.

They needn't have worried: Man Ray's admiration for everyday *objets trouvés* wasn't intended as a decorative Revolution, it was simply designed to draw attention to the fact that beauty is not only a matter of expensive materials and fine craftsmanship.

And it is this spirit, the understanding that a poor object can sit quite comfortably next to a priceless one, that the French have taken to heart and, typically, made their own.

It is also in this spirit that Patrick Guffraz's company, Lieux, launched their *art pauvre* collection. Designed by Guffraz and his former partner Philippe Renaud, each piece in the collection enjoys the same unpretentious and clever irony and wit that distinguished Man Ray's *objets* – particularly the lamps, devised from the simplest

ingredients: an upside-down goblet, a straight, thin rod of steel, a tiny cast bronze bunny, a casually twisted coil of wire … these lamps, when deconstructed, mean nothing, yet assembled, they are transformed into visually 'poetic' pieces. This is decoration by 'ideas and intellect', not by 'indulgence'.

The perfect showcase for Lieux's collection is Patrick Guffraz's own Paris apartment. Painted in a stunning shade of red throughout, the space is punctuated by the twisting, unpredictable and delicate shapes of Lieux's lamps. Topped by small shades in bright colours and *faux* patterns, they are in a sense the candelabras of the 20th century, the modern-day equivalent of 19th-century candlesticks. Small, lithe and unassuming in proportion, they reflect a trend that is quite noticeable in Paris today – a move away from large lamps and shades. These lamps, like Diego Giacometti's thin plaster columns, through their discretion allow a far more flexible role and usage in the interior. They can stand comfortably on a stack of books or sit on an unused chair. Formality is out, flexibility is in.

Interestingly, and without deliberate planning, most of the interiors photographed for this book turned out to have lamps from Lieux's *art pauvre* range. Perhaps in another couple of decades, a smart antiquarian will make a name by 'rediscovering' them.

PREVIOUS PAGE (74)
*Red became a firm favourite as one of the most 'French' colours because of two strong influences. First, the discovery of Pompeii and Herculaneum revealed the Roman and Greek love of colour. By way of the Grand Tour a shade known as Pompeian red captured the imagination of **Paris mondain**. Etruscan red, as it was also known, was synonymous with **le goût grec** – the taste for antiquity. Second, through trade with China and the Far East, Chinoiserie became all the rage in French and other European decorative circles: the Chinese saw red as the colour of contentment. Both these influences have had a strong and continuing effect on French taste. Red was the colour Patrick Guffraz*

chose as the decorative scheme for his Paris apartment.

PREVIOUS PAGES (76–77)
*Furnished simply, Guffraz's home is a discreet showcase for the designs of his company, Lieux. The coral and glass table was designed by Garouste and Bonnetti for Lieux and the lamps, with their small shades and playfully simple construction, are from a range designed by Philippe Renaud called **art pauvre** (literally, 'poor art'). There is a distinct trend in Paris at the moment towards small delicate lamps and equally subtle shades, no doubt a reflection once again of the fascination with the French 18th century. Candlesticks in the 18th century were always used with shades. Make-up in those days was all*

*wax-based and no self-respecting member of the **beau monde** would risk a facial meltdown.*

OPPOSITE PAGE
*A table-scape in Guffraz's home features one of the most popular Renaud designs from the **art pauvre** series. The 'rose branch in an amphora' lamp is almost a metaphor for all the qualities and characteristics that distinguish French taste. Classic in form (what could be more classic than an amphora and a thorny rose branch?), it is a reference to the ubiquitous taste for antiquity; elegant in proportion and materials, it reflects the French love of fine texture and form. And lastly, and just as important, it has daring and wit … classic and clever – the ultimate Parisian accolade.*

A

CONSTANT

CURIOSITY

It is not the production of beautiful objects alone that has surrounded the French arts with prestige for centuries. Perhaps more than anything it has also been the tension (a quintessential ingredient in art) between respect for tradition and a constant curiosity in search of innovation. This still applies today.

Denise Orsoni, presently the toast of Paris because of her distinctive 'style', is a great example of how the taste-making system works. An influential dealer and designer, she has made quite a name for herself with her 1940s discoveries. Perhaps because the decade was half taken up by a monstrous war, its decorative arts have never received much attention. As such, the creative work of these years, in furniture, textiles and decorative *objets*, has gone largely undiscovered.

By 1945, although France was on the side of the victors, the country had been ruined by years of war. The silver lining, as always, proved to be the pre-eminence of French craftsmanship. The excellence that had enabled leading Art Deco designers to experiment with form and colour in combinations of precious materials would now also facilitate the yearnings of postwar designers.

Not surprisingly, postwar 1940s design was reassuringly curvaceous, warm, soft and simple. A new look, described as 'freedom of form', led to the emergence of a style that was essentially a reaction against the conscious angularity of the 1930s. A preference for organic form and a taste for natural materials gave it the sensual, sophisticated signature that stimulated Denise Orsoni's interest and prompted a popular revival.

Orsoni began her career as an antique dealer specializing in French faïence, building up her reputation as 'the' source for exotic soup tureens and monumental cake plates by legendary names such as Dieulefit, Bonnefoy and St-Jean-du-Désert. Then one day, out of the blue, she'd had enough … no more matching tea sets, no more jam jars! Her new love was the style of the 1940s: Jean-Michel Frank's wicker boxes, Diego Giacometti's elegant plastercasts, the décors of André Arbus and exquisite creations by Venetian legend Mario Fortuny.

Orsoni set up a new shop a few doors down from the one she had only just closed. It was all new and fresh and she soon became the darling of the aesthetes. Azzedine Alaïa, Jacques Grange and all the other 'heavy hitters' in matters of taste in Paris applauded her vision and bought her 'fabulous finds'. Plaster, gilt and wrought iron, previously banished as 'bad taste', were suddenly revived.

Then, without warning, Orsoni once again demonstrated her contempt for cosy complacency. The sign on the door of her shop read '*Fermé pour cause de travaux*' (closed for works) – a nice touch! At the height of her success, Madame Orsoni went 'underground' … literally. She shifted her life, home, showroom and office into the vast catacombs of a windowless 17th-century cellar next to the Palais Royal. What were previously the rat infested kitchens of a restaurant were now to be home to the collections of one of Paris's sharpest taste-makers. Despite doubts and reservations from even her staunchest supporters, Orsoni went ahead with her catacomb conversion. A pipe was brought in to provide 'fresh' Paris air, candles replaced daylight, alcoves were converted into cosy bedchambers and sumptuous velvets were wrapped around the pipes that run along most of the cellar ceilings. In the course of further early-morning raids on the flea markets, she was able to find and combine 19th-century *toile de Jouy*, Fortuny velvets, circa 1900 hat stands made into lamps, the strong, simple lines of furniture designed by Art Deco architect Francis Jourdain and a 1900s table covered in a replica of a third-century Syrian mosaic. And with typically Parisian curiosity for the new she commissioned pieces from a young German cabinet-maker named Toby Schumann.

In the capable hands of Denise Orsoni all these fabulous finds combine exquisitely to create an 'under-wonder-world'. For the same money it could have been a cellar full of junk. It is this very French notion of 'tension', of constantly being on the 'edge' between the experimental and the plain crazy, that gives this city its unique sense of style.

PREVIOUS PAGE (80)
*A **tulipière** made by Denise Orsoni, reproduced from a 1940s original, is indicative of the individual signature she has brought to the Paris design scene: a signature based on the décors of André Arbus, the sculptural simplicity of Giacometti plastercasts and the textural talent of Jean-Michel Frank. No less unique is the venue she has chosen as showroom and home: a cav-ernous vault, a cellar that was once the kitchen of a fashionable restaurant, devoid of daylight, near the Palais Royal in the centre of Paris.*

OPPOSITE PAGE
Guests are entertained in a tented dining room made from 1940s fabrics found at the flea markets. The dining chairs are upholstered in Fortuny fabrics (circa 1940), the table is inlaid with a mosaic copied from a third-century Syrian villa, and the 18th-century Provençal buffet displays a faïence tureen from Dieulefit and candlesticks made from hat stands. The fashion for tented dining rooms was first introduced at the time of Napoleon's campaigns into Egypt and Italy. People were captivated by the romantic notion of their heroic General waging war and living in a tent, and soon no important house in Paris was without one.

1	2	3	4
5	6	7	8

PHOTOS IN ORDER OF
APPEARANCE – PREVIOUS PAGES (84–85)

1

Spiral stairs that used to lead from the restaurant to the subterranean kitchen now provide a theatrical descent into Denise Orsoni's cavernous cellar/showroom/home.

2

French velvet from the 1940s is draped along the ceiling to disguise unsightly pipes and an oak chair, a pseudo-Renaissance flea market find, sits on top of an African-inspired rug – also from the 1940s.

3

Wrought-iron candelabras, original packing crates for tea from India, oversize faïence pieces such as the massive water jug and furniture adorned with 1940s fabrics are the hallmarks of Orsoni's style, even in the kitchen.

4

The substantial vault-like entrance door, upholstered in her signature jute, is reminiscent of 1940s designer Jean-Michel Frank's taste for luxurious, tactile natural fibres.

5

A 1930s sofa upholstered in jute with gilded feet, reproduced to order by Orsoni, is flanked by a couple of metal spheres (which used to be marine buoys) on plinths. The standing lamp is a Fortuny 'Beehive' light.

6

Arched alcoves off the main cellar were well suited to their use as bedrooms. The late 1940s wooden bed is by renowned French designer Francis Jourdain, the sculpted relief on the partition wall is by Terzieff and storage is taken care of with recycled shop fittings.

7

Orsoni's underworld cellar has enough space for a salon, two bedrooms, a dining room and an office/study. A terracotta wall lamp and a typically Parisian iron bottle rack continue the flea market and '40s signature.

8

Before settling in to her present preoccupation with French 1940s design, Orsoni was passionate about, and an expert in, French faïence, preferably 18th century. Not surprisingly, she has used every niche and gap in the place, such as this old delivery chute, to display some of her pieces

0PPOSITE PAGE

Illuminated by a 1940s plaster-cast light fitting, one of many that Orsoni found, a marble trough perched on a pair of stone columns is used as a plant holder, an unexpected sight in a place that gets no daylight.

2

ORIGINS

None of us exists in a vacuum. Everything about us, where we live and how we live, is inextricably linked to how our forebears lived. Connected to our ancestors via distinct forms, patterns, rhythms and shapes, we belong to societies that are in a continuing balancing act between forging forward and looking back. We cannot escape history and tradition.

1

The triumphal arch of the Porte Saint-Denis (named after the first French bishop, beheaded by the Romans in AD 250) was built in 1672 by Louis XIV to celebrate his military victories. He demolished Charles V's city walls and created a swathe of leafy promenades. In place of the city gates, a series of triumphal arches were planned: this and the neighbouring Porte Saint-Martin were the first.

2

Parisians built monuments even to the most mundane necessities. This artesian well in the Place de Breteuil was dug in 1833–41 and supplied the whole of the Left Bank with drinking water. The tower was designed by Delaporte and stretched 130 feet into the air. It was demolished in 1903.

3

Hôtel des Invalides, recently regilded to mark the bicentenary of the Revolution, was originally built by Louis XIV as a home for invalided soldiers. The dome houses two churches: one for the soldiers and one intended as a mausoleum for the King – it was Napoleon, however, who was instead laid to rest here.

4

At the centre of Place Vendôme, Napoleon stands high on the Colonne de la Grande Armée, a monumental column clad with relief bronze plates cast from the remains of 1200 cannons captured from the Austrians. The plates depict scenes of 'trophies' being taken from the enemy. The inspiration for the column is attributed to Baron Denon, Napoleon's counsellor for the arts.

5

Place de la République is one of the largest roundabouts in Paris. It was designed as the pivotal point in Haussmann's grand scheme. In the middle is a statue of the Republic, with the figures of Liberty, Equality and Fraternity, by the brothers Morice. The bronze reliefs around the base are by Dalou.

6

Louis XV's act of gratitude to Sainte Geneviève, patron saint of Paris, for curing him of a serious illness was to build what is now known as the Panthéon, a domed and porticoed church in the classical style situated in the heart of the Latin Quarter. The Revolution converted it into a mausoleum for the great.

7

'Our generation's mission is to complete the French Revolution,' declared Gambetta in 1869. Gambetta was a mobilizing force, organizing opposition to Napoleon III's oppressive regime, and a symbol of the nation's struggle when he flew out of Paris by hot air balloon on 19 September 1870 in an effort to rally troops in the countryside to break the Prussian siege of Paris.

8

Napoleon's Arc de Triomphe du Carroussel, modelled on the arch of Septimius Severus in Rome, was built at the then enormous cost of ten million francs. It is another example of the monumental constructions erected over the centuries by kings and emperors to propagate French power and prestige.

0 PPOSITE PAGE

Place de la Bastille at night. Although the power of the central monument – actually built in remembrance of the three days of streetfighting in 1830 when Charles V was deposed – has been somewhat diffused by the new opera house, the square is still the rallying area for political protesters.

MAN RAY

AND THE

FOUND

OBJECT

Throughout history, the French have shown a particular penchant for reinventing, or sometimes simply for recreating, the past, particularly in the decorative arts.

Marie Antoinette had a taste for the style of ancient Rome, as did her ill-fated husband Louis XVI and his predecessors Louis XV and Louis XIV. Napoleon, too, was fascinated by the immaculate proportions of classical Rome and the monumental structures and icons of ancient Egypt. In turn, the Empress Eugénie, the wife of Napoleon III, identified with Marie Antoinette and led a revival of late 18th-century Louis XVI style. Even Art Deco, touted as something new, could be seen as a return to the *luxe* and dazzling craftsmanship of the Empire period.

French taste has often run the risk of reviving itself to death. This was particularly so in the late 19th century, when unbridled romanticism led to the simultaneous revival of just about every phase of French history, good or bad. Department stores produced catalogues offering bad copies of questionable items from every period from Henri IV to Louis XVI. Tradition can be a creative force in the decorative arts, bringing experience to bear in the design process, but it can also get in the way of innovation when the maintenance of traditional values becomes an end in itself.

Luckily, the odd rebel has ensured an occasional injection of the radical and new. Man Ray, an American artist who spent most of his adult life in Paris, fought the 'blind attraction' to technical skill and craftsmanship. He was not against such qualities *per se*, but he did not think they should be the exclusive criteria by which we judge beauty. He introduced the beauty of the everyday: a discarded shoe, an empty match-box, a plain iron, even a baguette and a pair of scales could constitute an *objet d'art*.

In a society nurtured on notions of grandeur and *luxe*, he was a cat among the decorative pigeons. He was a radical, but he wasn't alone. Magritte, Duchamp and Picasso were also masters at turning 'worthless junk' into items of wit and beauty.

There is no greater vindication of the manner in which Man Ray elevated the status of the 'humble, absurd and yet often beautiful objects which are part of our everyday lives', as his biographer Roland Penrose puts it, than the art world's response to his widow's auction. Man Ray was an 'indefatigable forager' and his studio was

always choc-a-bloc with the trophies of the street scavenger. He would paste a portrait of Picasso on an old matchbox and fill it with paper clips, arrange a couple of mattress springs on a stand, balance timber mannequins on an old bottle rack, turn a shoebox into a homage to a friend, glue a shoe sole to a cheap frame, and so on. Yet at a Sotheby's auction in 1994 following the death of his widow Juliet, the prices paid for these objects were, in many instances, far higher than those for the most beautifully made antiques. It was a triumph of intellect over convention.

Man Ray would probably have thought the whole 'performance' absurd and it would no doubt have confirmed his cynical suspicions about the world. Far more important, however, than the price fetched by his *Peint Bleu* is the freedom this work restored to the melting pot of French taste. Suddenly it was okay again to slip a kitsch postcard of a Spanish dancer next to a little Rubens, or to surround a precious 'bronze' with shiny green apples.

PREVIOUS PAGE (98)
Although best known for his innovative photography, Man Ray, perhaps more than any other Parisian artist, legitimized the notion of the found object as art. In a corner of his widow's apartment, 'It's Springtime', two mattress springs twisted together, is arranged with a small bronze entitled 'Hermaphrodite' – one of his sculptures from 1919. The black and white snapshot is of his wife Juliet standing next to his most famous 'phallic' sculpture, the 1920 'Priapus Paperweight' – two steel balls and a tube, a light-hearted homage to the male genitals.

PREVIOUS PAGES (100–101)
Man Ray was a lifelong hoarder. The collection he accumulated in his studio was vast and certainly too big for the apartment

Juliet took after his death. On display is an edited version of all his 'stuff' by the last and perhaps most loved woman in his life. Along one wall are 'Céleste est à l'Est de l'Ouest', a portrait of Juliet, formerly a dancer, and a bust entitled 'Marquis de Sade', a figure with whom Man Ray strongly identified as an example of the ultimate libertarian. The photograph on the canvas shopping bag and the poster is one of his most famous. Today it can be found on everything from bags to coffee cups.

PREVIOUS PAGES (102–103)
Reclining on the floor of Juliet's apartment, suitably framed by a black carpet, is the full-size plaster model of a sculpture entitled 'Hermaphrodite', which he first conceived in 1919. Man Ray was always much

more concerned with the value of an idea than the date of a work's first creation, so many pieces were done again after the original attempt had been lost or destroyed. He didn't appreciate the art world's obsession with dates: 'I'm not a wine,' he would remark.

OPPOSITE PAGE
Along one wall in the apartment, Juliet arranged Man Ray's famous 'Still Lifes in a Box' series. A bust surrounded with newspaper is a self-portrait from 1932. His objects, as he would say, were 'designed to amuse, bewilder, annoy or inspire reflection, but never to arouse admiration for any technical excellence' – a sharp dig at the obsession of traditional 'French taste' with quality, precision and grandeur.

3

COLOURS

Colour plays a distinct role in shaping the visual culture of a city or country. It is one of the oldest forms of communication known, and we are attracted to it like magpies to a shiny object. Colour is simple and pure.

MADAME DE

POMPADOUR'S

PINK

AND OTHER DELICACIES

The colours of Paris are every bit as complex and intriguing as the history of Paris itself. Each important epoch of the French decorative arts has a chromatic equivalent.

If the 18th century, for example, could be defined by a single 'chromatic caption', it would be white with gold. Influenced by the Italian Renaissance, French interiors were exquisitely grand, and the participants in court life prided themselves on their refinement in all aspects of life. The backdrops to all this splendour were intricately panelled chambers, painted white, detailed in gilding. Both the Sun King and his successor Louis XV were smugly self-satisfied at their 'taste', secure in the knowledge that Andrea Palladio himself had said that 'white is particularly satisfying to God'. Their style had thus been given the divine stamp of approval by the acknowledged expert.

Such a simple pairing has proved to be one of the strongest influences in the French decorative arts. Time and time again the classic combination of white and gold has been dragged out of the historical cupboard, dusted off and copied. The Empress Eugénie, wife of Napoleon III, reintroduced the fashion for white panelled rooms with gilded detailing. Even today, it remains the epitome of classic *chic*. Hubert de Givenchy, sophisticated couturier for the elite, has a Paris apartment in which he combines the white and gold of the *ancien régime* with pared-down modern design.

Not that the 18th century was without colour. In fact, one of the single greatest events to influence the historical perception of colour occurred in the 1760s after the excavation of Pompeii. The discovery of the incredibly well-preserved ruins of Herculaneum and Pompeii provided scholars with the first accurate window on the civilization of ancient Rome and revealed a totally unexpected sophistication, including a colouring expertise which completely overturned the notion of the 'all-white' Roman Empire. Scrapings from the 'original' paints revealed a use of deep reds, brilliant blues, sumptuous yellows and rich greens.

These colours made their way into the fashionable repertoire of French society. Even the Revolution didn't hinder the growth in influence of 'neo-classical' colour because the Revolutionaries welcomed the association with the nobler principles of Roman civilization. By the time Napoleon came to power, Pompeian red, Naples yellow, pea green and cerulean blue were an essential part of the French palette.

In his quest for the colours that would project the prestige of his rule, Napoleon added Egyptian and Prussian blue to the chromatic mix. Egyptian blue, a bright vivid blue, was based on observations made during his campaigns in Egypt where this particular colour was used by the locals to paint doors and shutters in an effort to distract evil spirits. Prussian blue, a deep, cool blue that was actually the first true chemical dye, made from a compound of ferro-cyanide (hence cyan), was called 'Prussian' because it was discovered in 1704 in Berlin, the capital of Prussia. Commercially available from 1724, its formula was as zealously guarded by the Prussians as any military secret. Napoleon was a great admirer of this strong, masculine shade. So much so that when access was restricted in response to his own military aggression, he announced a prize for the first person in France to discover a way to make blue without using indigo (the traditional source). It was probably the first time in history that a world ruler had been held to ransom by a colour. The British controlled most of the world's indigo production out of India and the Germans held the 'chemical secret' of making blue; both were using embargoes and blockades as military adjuncts.

The 'Continental Blockade' also prompted Napoleon to establish a course in industrial chemistry and dyes in Lyons, the centre of the silk-weaving industry. This, allied with the growth of the luxury industries, produced a host of colour-related innovations later in the century. The glass industries, for example, introduced many new colours into their repertoire, such as vivid yellow, derived from uranium. Porcelain, increasingly desirable to the new moneyed classes, also introduced a kaleidoscope of new tints. By the time of the Second Empire, 'French taste' had been enriched by the possibilities of an extraordinarily broad palette of colour choices, including the soft, sophisticated shades of the pre-Revolutionary aristocracy, such as the favourite pink of Louis XV's long-time mistress, Madame de Pompadour, resurrected by the Empress Eugénie, a great fan of La Pompadour.

Colour, thus, has played an integral part in the evolution of France. The significance of particular colours makes them meaningful as ingredients … In Paris, to paint a room is to invoke history.

PREVIOUS PAGE (108)
'Pompadour pink' refers to the pretty shade of pink that was one of Madame de Pompadour's favourite colours. It is used here for the quirky storage drawers and cabinets in the dressing room of Florence Dostal's Montparnasse studio.

Pompoms (no pun intended) as drawer pulls reflect Dostal's typically French love of 'folly'.

OPPOSITE PAGE
Red, green and yellow were the favourite colours of Napoleon's Empire, and pea green was the most popular shade of green.

This 18th-century colour has become a staple of the French interior decoration repertoire. The pea-green door photographed here is decorated with a hotchpotch of things that reflect the French love of combining the freewheeling, the ephemeral and the nostalgic.

1

*With yellow and red, green is one of the main colours of neo-classicism. The pea green of this door is a staple of the French interior repertoire. As with red, it is very difficult to achieve the right shade, which is why a shade like pea green endows a room with a certain **hauteur**.*

2

*White and gold are the colours of the French 18th century. Acres of stately **châteaux** and **appartements de parade** attest to this taste for white panelled suites finished with gilded detailing. Once the exclusive domain of the French aristocracy, white and gold remain associated to this day with the **ancien régime**.*

3

Gustavian grey is another shade associated with neo-classicism. Named after King Gustavus of Sweden, grey was a deliberately sober choice for interiors. Neo-classicism was about restraint; it was also a 'masculine' movement, and so this rather refined shade, without a hint of matronly affectation, fitted the bill perfectly.

4

Pink, particularly the crisp, bright, acidic tone shown here, was favoured by Madame de Pompadour, Marie Antoinette and the Empress Eugénie. Combined with gilding and touches of silver, it imparted a distinctly French quality to the interiors in which it was used.

5

***Bleu de porcelaine**, a light cerulean blue, has been immortalized in the French decorative arts as a result of its adoption by the porcelain industry. Known in England as 'Wedgwood blue', this particular hue has remained a favourite for interiors ever since it was first used for decorative highlighting on bone china.*

6

Red, the hue of contentment in China, has long been a French decorative favourite, especially after the discoveries at Pompeii which established terracotta red as a colour favoured by Roman antiquity. Deep, saturated reds, such as Pompeian red and Etruscan red, became popular choices for interiors, particularly dining rooms.

7

Naples yellow, another vivid neo-classical tint, was one of Napoleon's favourite colours. Based on a discovery made in the ruins of Pompeii and Herculaneum, it was used as a background to many of the Emperor's most heroic interiors, such as at Malmaison.

8

Prussian blue was one of the colours Napoleon chose to represent the grandeur of his Empire, specifying its use in everything from the decorative band on the Imperial porcelain to the upholstery of the mahogany chairs in his official suites. He attached the same prestige to Prussian blue that ancient Rome had to purple.

O
PPOSITE PAGE

Napoleon's Egyptian campaign, and the subsequent programmes that were established to study the culture of this ancient land, created an important chromatic addition to popular style with the introduction of 'Egyptian blue', a bright blue that became a favourite of Regency as well as Empire style.

4
INGREDIENTS

Design is like a language. It is often specific to a place and its overall culture. The same symbols and patterns resurface in different forms and styles and they serve as both the source and the result of creative inspiration.

CREATIVE

CARDBOARD

It was in a shop in New York. SoHo to be exact. The place was French and it was filled with beautiful things. Elegant scrubbed tables, handsome chairs, candlesticks, the ubiquitous Provençal *armoire*, and there on the wall, completely at home in its surroundings, was what looked like an 18th-century portrait in a heavily gilded ornate frame. It was a fake. Both the portrait and the frame were made of cardboard. Why would someone of such obvious artistic ability go to all that trouble to make something so intricate … in cardboard? The shop owner didn't understand the question. It was beautiful, was it not? Well, then, why not? She was French.

As the Duc de Choiseul, court minister of Louis XV, said: 'We have no rules about anything. Rules are like shackles, pleasure cannot abide them.'

He was a man of his word. When Louis XV, in the aftermath of some bloody court intrigue, approached his minister and said, 'Cousin, we no longer have need of your services', the Duc de Choiseul was banished to his country estate. Once there, he continued with all the inventive parties and *soirées* that had made him such a popular character. All his friends from court made the journey to attend. Louis XV did not want them to go but he also did not forbid it, so they went. Eventually, the Duc's popularity was such that the King had to allow him back. As a gesture of appreciation to all his friends, Choiseul built the famous *folie*, 'le pagode de Chanteloup', a four-storey Chinese-inspired pagoda. Set in exquisite gardens, it is now protected as a national monument.

It was a gesture of such elegant eccentricity; exactly the kind of which the French are most fond.

Throughout history, in matters of taste and style the French have celebrated the *folie* with heartfelt enthusiasm. It is the very soul of the French decorative arts.

From Marie Antoinette's completely absurd Laiterie to Cocteau's grass-covered walls, the eccentric, the overdone and the completely *fou* have always had great cachet. The same still hold true today.

Thus it is quite *sympathique* that Amélie Dillemann should choose to create in cardboard. Yet it wasn't as if she deliberately set out to be different. She originally

THE

LEGEND

OF

AUBUSSON

The Palais des Tuileries, Château de Malmaison, Hôtel de Bourienne, Château de Fontainebleau, Hôtel de Beauharnais, the Louvre, Château de Saint-Cloud, the Elysée, Château de Compiègne, Hôtel de Charost ... all of these Empire residences, and more, were luxuriously furnished with acres of velvety Aubusson rugs by Napoleon. He loved the rugs from this small village in the middle of France. In 1806 alone, he is reputed to have spent three million francs at the Aubusson workshops. It is perhaps difficult to imagine this great ruler taking time off from his busy schedule of campaigning and conquering to look at fabric swatches, dye lots and design choices for rugs and carpets for his various homes. Yet for him, art, industry and politics were entirely connected. Traditional values that were inherited from the *ancien régime*, such as fine workmanship, respect for materials and refinement of detail and finish, were now integrated into the expanding luxury industries of France. With Napoleon's support, Aubusson produced items of unassailable beauty and quality, which in turn led to export and economic growth.

Long before the rugs that Napoleon so admired became *de rigueur*, Aubusson, a small village nestling on the banks of the Creuse, so well suited to the dyeing of wool with its ready supply of sparkling clean water, had a reputation for its exquisite tapestries. From the 14th century on, no nobleman's home was complete without an Aubusson tapestry stretching the entire length of at least one wall. Louis XIV, XV, XVI, Madame de Pompadour and Marie Antoinette were all clients of the workshops. Aubusson has always enjoyed a rather grand reputation, but the financial fate of this small town's workshops has been somewhat less consistent.

Long acclaimed as a centre for tapestry, the carpet factories were not established until 1743, when demand for Turkish and Persian carpets was such that supply could not be met. Shrewd marketing eyes spotted an opportunity and special workshops were created to make 'Oriental copies' for an increasingly comfort-obsessed high society. The women of the town were put to work in these new factories behind specially designed vertical looms 'so as not to entail too much bending forward, thought harmful to the female organs'. Not that healthcare or worker satisfaction were high on the list of priorities in those days. Monsieur Bonneval, the King's 'Inspector of Royal Manufactories', reported that families subsisted on nothing more than 'cabbage water soup and husk-ridden bread' and that they were forced to work hideously long hours, with lamps strung around their necks so that they could continue after daylight. When they did finally retire it was to straw beds in miserable hovels. The glamour was in the end-product, certainly not in the process.

Although the workshops of Aubusson were supremely skilled in manufacture, they were too far removed from their customers to be able to read the changing whims and fashions of the aristocracy. Demand for Aubusson carpets at court was on the decline by 1750: it fancied something altogether more French than Oriental copies and the workshops were slow to react. The moneyed middle classes thus became their new market. Aubusson's fate has remained variable: revival under Napoleon, the Industrial Revolution, the rug no longer being regarded by potential purchasers as the centrepiece in their decorative schemes. Survival has not been easy.

Despite a lot of effort in the early part of the 20th century to encourage design contributions from some of the most acclaimed contemporary artists, the traditional business of this town continues today in one workshop only. In a romantic, fairy-tale conclusion to the saga, the present proprietor, Jean-Jacques-Benedict Wattel, of the 'Manufacture Royale St Jean', has managed to make good a family dream. Monsieur Wattel's grandfather, a gentleman named Blondeau, was a painter who, in the best tradition of Aubusson's artists in residence, would paint the 'cartoons' for the carpets. His wife stood at the loom, giving life to her husband's designs. Together, they dreamt of one day owning the workshop. Their grandchild succeeded.

And Wattel is determined to reinstate the role of the handmade carpet in the French decorative arts. He is full of ideas. On the practical side he has greatly reduced the complexity of manufacture by paring down the number of different individual colour yarns, and on the marketing side he is busy forging relationships with high-profile designers such as Garouste and Bonnetti. More than 250 years ago, Aubusson got started in the rug business by identifying a gap in the market – who is to say that this won't happen again?

PREVIOUS PAGE (126)
A still life of an Aubusson tapestry and some scissors and spools recall the composition and light of the works of Dutch Masters – a not inappropriate comparison since Aubus-

son tapestries and rugs were around in the 17th century.

OPPOSITE PAGE
When Jean-Jacques Wattel took over the famed Aubusson workshop, he inherited a stock-

room with an extraordinary selection of spools of silk and wool. Almost like the equivalent of a life-size paint colour card, the spools reflect the detail and nuance that Aubusson rugs and tapestries were capable of.

where creation evolved into a healthy opposition between the old and the new. A contest developed between the the French tradition of the luxury trades, produced on an industrial scale, and the artist working on a personal scale. And it is this system, of sorts, that ensures that neither tradition or innovation is lost. The French decorative arts need input from houses such as Hermès, Zuber, Lalique, Daum, Baccarat *et al*, but they also thrive on the efforts of individuals such as Marc Bankowsky.

Working alone in a studio converted from the former cellars of a house just off Place Pigalle, Marc Bankowsky, who, like Amélie Dillemann, cut his creative teeth working in advertising, makes mirrors, sconces, hanging lamps and other *objets* in plaster, bronze, clay and even fibreglass. Like Art Nouveau, his style owes much to the inspiration of the 'Vegetable Kingdom'.

His penchant for natural shapes is evident in his tea cups moulded from real maple leaves, in a wall light that imitates the texture and colour of a lemon and in a fibreglass screen that perfectly mimics generous folds of fabric. It is a style that celebrates and explores the romance of nature and it seems perfectly appropriate that his house, smack in the middle of the area of Paris associated with the Belle Epoque of Toulouse-Lautrec, should at one time have been in the countryside.

It is in a *cul de sac* surrounded by artist's ateliers that previously belonged to such illustrious residents as Braque and Dufy; the area is now a bizarre combination of neon lights, sex shops and peep shows. This mix of contemporary reality and historic associations is what provides such a rich *milieu* for creativity. Undeniably contemporary and highly individual, Bankowsky's work nevertheless reflects the influence of his surroundings and their corresponding history and ambience.

One day, in true French style, the creative circuit will be completed when Bankowsky is asked to design pieces for one or perhaps several of the aforementioned traditional luxury manufacturers. In the meantime, Marc Bankowsky is completely at home in this bizarre quarter of Paris with his small son Louis, his cat Marcel, Bach and Mozart – and his own romantic, nature-inspired creations.

PREVIOUS PAGE (134)
Examples of Marc Bankowsky's work sparkle on his own mantelpiece. A plaster frame intended for a mirror, a leaf-shaped candlestick and a lemon wall lamp of moulded plastic are his latest works. The shapes and textures of nature are the primary inspiration.

PREVIOUS PAGES (136–137)
The bedroom is dominated by a fibreglass moulded screen that perfectly mimics the folds of draped fabric, natural linen sheets and a turn-of-the-century café chair. Bankowsky's personal signature for his interior can best be described as romantic minimalism.

OPPOSITE PAGE
Painted a deep shade of blue reminiscent of Majorelle blue, an open courtyard has been re-modelled as an interior atrium. Playful Moroccan-style arches contrast with the serious plaster bust of the great Condé, which was purchased from the Paris castmaker Lorenzi.

5

VIRTUOSI

In music, in art, in almost every human creative endeavour, there are always people who stand out, people whose achievements warrant focus and attention. They often establish new directions and create pioneering approaches; they are leaders – they are the virtuosi in their chosen field of expertise.

THE

TACTILE

DESIGN

OF

CHRISTIAN ASTUGUEVIEILLE

It is only fitting that a book devoted to the found object and its role in Parisian style should conclude with a look at the future. Thus, this chapter is devoted to the extraordinary design work of Christian Astuguevieille, a man who actually makes 'found objects', new pieces enriched with what he describes as 'imaginary meaning for the imaginary man'.

In a world that has lost touch with ritual meaning, he is busy making modern-day totems, objects and furniture that are less concerned with function and more with communication. 'Touch' and 'feel' are important words in the Astuguevieille vocabulary. Early in his career he worked with children who had elocution problems, instructing their teachers how to get through to them; *communicate*. For five years he directed the children's studio and gallery at the Centre Pompidou, working with ideas of tactility and space and how the two relate.

Given his fascination with touch and its relation to art and the object, it's perhaps not surprising that Astuguevieille's own work began with jewelry. His modern tribal creations were an immediate success and soon no couture show in Paris was complete without his jewelry to adorn it. Fashion houses were quick to spot his talent. Astuguevieille's ability to stimulate what he himself describes as 'a well-buried primal response' led to his eventual appointment as creative director of the house of Rochas.

It was in these first years at Rochas that his work began to draw the attention of the design community. Initially, it was his own home that stole the limelight. It is a classic Parisian apartment, *un appartement de parade*, straight out of the Chanel ads for Egoïste perfume. High ceilings, parquet floors, marble fireplaces, tall, elegant windows and exquisite detailing distinguish a space that would even look good empty. What he then did with it was even more remarkable. With no regard for convention, he made it timeless – at once minimal, primal and delicate.

Single leaves were elegantly framed in a succession of ebony boxes, and his books were wrapped in exotic textiles, tied with the *Furoshiki* knot, a traditional technique

143

To call Astuguevieille a furniture designer, however, would be selling him short. He is an artist with a distinctive vision. He is like Brancusi in that, for all that his approach is so singular, it can go so many different ways. Despite his visual discipline, or precisely because of it, Brancusi was able to steer his work in many directions. He worked in timber, in stone, in bronze, and, had he been allowed to, he would have built what would then have been the world's tallest tower in Chicago, a gigantic version of his geometric hourglass sculpture towers, the 'endless columns'.

Astuguevieille has not ventured into architecture yet, but it is entirely conceivable that he will. His work is so distinctive in concept and appearance that it is not hard to picture a building wound round with cord (or perhaps steel cable), adorned with intricate swirls, knots and spirals … a 'monumental' totem pole for an urban tribe starved of visual poetry and meaning.

Hopefully it will be as controversial as the Eiffel Tower, the Centre Pompidou and I.M. Pei's glass pyramid were in their own day – and as successful.

PREVIOUS PAGES (148–149)
*In his large kitchen Astugue-vieille demonstrates his skill at interior design. A rich tableau of the type of **objets** that make a kitchen an inviting place to eat as well as to cook in is a result of his collection of simple white crockery and impressively scaled glass as well as the natural and neutral simplicity of his furniture.*

OPPOSITE PAGE
Astuguevieille's most recent work is quite bizarre. A fake Louis XV commode is covered in shreds of white cord, which are then trimmed like the pile of a rug. The result is a piece that at first glance looks like a valuable

antique that has been tarred and feathered. A witty comment on the Revolution? Or a natural progression? Perhaps both.

FOLLOWING PAGE (152)
A view of a study corner in Astuguevieille's apartment is a testament to the versatility and scope of his creativity. He manages to find enough permutations within his own oeuvre to decorate his entire apartment and to keep a full-time shop. Man Ray was right … it's the strength of the idea that counts.

FOLLOWING PAGE (153)
Primitivism is instantly recognizable in the design: it is human, heroic and poetic –

a reaction against the overly processed. The undictated, the rediscovered and the untold story are the mysteries that Astuguevieille hopes to instil in his design. Touch, he says, is essential to life; its tenderness is felt from our earliest contact with the world, when we are born. The way things feel is most important to Christian Astuguevieille,

FOLLOWING PAGE (154)
Constructed in a similar fashion to the commode shown on page 151, this club chair definitely has what author Barbara Stoeltie describes as 'a vegetable quality; you can't resist caressing the surreal, shaggy stuff'.

"In whatever form the object is finally presented,
by a drawing, by a painting, by a photograph or by the object itself,
it is designed to amuse, bewilder, annoy or inspire reflection,
but not to arouse admiration for any technical excellence
usually sought in other works of art."

Man Ray

ACKNOWLEDGMENTS

Quite simply, this book wouldn't have been possible without the contribution of René and Barbara Stoeltie – not just because they are tirelessly devoted to the discovery and photography of the most interesting people and their homes, but because, after living in Amsterdam, Brussels, London and Prague, they have ultimately chosen to settle in Paris. They understand what the art of living in Paris is all about because they are part of it. It is this 'hometown' advantage that they bring to this book, the ability to experience Paris from a local's perspective without losing the awe and innocence of the visitor, which is, I believe, necessary to appreciate the city's visual splendour fully. René's photographs and Barbara's research reflect the real Paris, a city famous for its diversity and variety, yet held together by a strong sense of cultural similarity and uniformity. My only regret is that we only had 160 pages available: so many beautiful and spectacular photos ended up, alas, on the cutting room floor.

BIBLIOGRAPHY

Boyer, Marie-France. *Paris Style*. London: Weidenfeld & Nicolson, 1989.

Calloway, Stephen. *Baroque Baroque*. London: Phaidon, 1994.

–––. *Twentieth-Century Decoration*. London: Weidenfeld & Nicolson, 1988.

Deschamps, Madeleine. *Empire*. London: Booth Clibborn Editions, 1994.

Downey, Claire. *Neo-Furniture*. London: Thames and Hudson, 1992.

Eriksen, Svend. *Early Neo-Classicism in France*. London: Faber & Faber, 1974.

Fiell, Charlotte and Peter. *Modern Furniture Classics since 1945*. London: Thames and Hudson, 1991.

Fleischmann, Melanie, and Mick Hales. *In the Neo-Classic Style*. London: Columbus Books, 1988.

Gilliat, Mary. *The Blue and White Room*. New York: Bantam Books, 1992.

McFadden, David. *L'Art de Vivre: Decorative Arts and Design in France 1789–1989*. London: Thames and Hudson, 1989.

Newman, Bruce M. *Fantasy Furniture*. New York: Rizzoli, 1989.

Penrose, Roland. *Man Ray*. London: Thames and Hudson, 1975.

Thornton, Peter. *Authentic Decor*. London: Weidenfeld & Nicolson, 1984.

GILDED

CANDLESTICK

Candlesticks have always played a substantial role in the domestic affairs of the French home. Despite the introduction of electricity, the candelabra continues to be a sought-after item. This one, designed by Roberto Bergero, unites the decorative influences of nature in the organic shape that mimics coral, another popular sea shape and the 18th-century preference for gilding and the sense of **folie** *so central to the Parisian distaste for pretension. Made from moulded plaster and decorated with pearls, it is yet another example of the increasing influence of* **art pauvre.**

Tel. 33 1 42626878

SOLO

STARFISH

Gilles Dufour, creative director of the house of Chanel and right-hand man for Karl Lagerfeld, used starfish, painted red and stuck on at random, to decorate his pale yellow walls. The humble starfish is one of the best examples of an **objet trouvé.** *Eclectic, organic, eccentric, simple and unpretentious, it fulfils all the roles: no wonder the French love this oceanic anomaly. It is the sublime 'mistake'; the piece of oddball inspiration that is considered so vital to the success of an interior. And it is not the only sea creature that appears in Parisian interiors. Shells and pearls also adorn the odd* **objet d'art.**

The best source for crustacean creatures is the Conran Shop Tel. 44 171 589 7401

FRENCH

FORTIES DESIGN

At the end of the Second World War, angular lines and bold geometric shapes, the signatures of French 1930s style, were replaced by a taste for comfortable curves and reassuring simplicity. Forties design was all about sumptuous sensuality, which was not altogether surprising given the bleak years that had preceded. Yet this postwar period of design was a dormant memory until Parisian taste-maker Denise Orsoni woke the Paris **beau monde** *with her 1940s finds. This* **tulipière,** *modelled on an original found in her regular forays to the Paris flea markets, is one of many pieces that have sparked a fresh interest in the design of the 1940s.*

Available from David Gill Tel. 44 171 589 5946

BALLOON

WALL LAMP

Ever since the Montgolfier brothers, the paper manufacturers who invented the hot-air balloon, amazed and delighted the crowds attending the first Paris exhibition in 1801 with their invention, **Montgolfières,** *as they are called in France, have featured prominently in the French arts as a decorative icon. Florence Dostal continues the tradition. Wall lamps mimic the typical bunches of balloons from parks and fairgrounds. Yet despite the* **folie** *of the design, Dostal does not treat the quality of manufacture as a joke. Her kooky ideas are entrusted only to the finest glass-blowers and artisans of Murano.*

Liberty Tel. 44 171 734 1234 or Heals's Tel. 44 171 636 1666

PLASTER

WALL LAMP

*Following an artistic tradition initiated by Diego Giacometti, brother of the famous sculptor, plaster lamps, moulded in a whimsical and witty manner, have found their way into the hearts and homes of Parisians. Legendary figures of the French interior design world, such as the late Jean-Michel Frank, have given this poor material genuine status through the addition of sculptural pieces to the French interior. Satisfying the need for **folie** and the dislike of bourgeois pretension, lamps moulded from plaster are, following a significant period of exile, back in favour. These hands are from the **art pauvre** range of Lieux, Patrick Guffraz's company.*

Tel. 33 1 42785771

NOUVEAU

ART NOUVEAU

Inspired by the forms, shapes and textures of nature, designer Marc Bankowsky makes objects that recall the decorative force that so influenced the short-lived Art Nouveau movement. Lush with floral and natural motifs, Art Nouveau was a tribute to the fabulous aspects of nature being discovered in the French colonies. It was also the first decorative movement, as Le Corbusier would put it, to 'shake off the garments of an old culture'. Free of historical precedent, Art Nouveau was entirely contemporary, a close parallel to Bankowsky's work today. Bronze door handles in the shape of leafy branches reveal his penchant for natural shapes and the way in which he uses the vegetable kingdom in a modern, minimal manner.

Marc Bankowsky can be contacted on 33 1 42543078

BAROQUE

BUST

Design author Stephen Calloway describes Oriel Harwood's work as 'objects that evoke the sense of wonder that the finest artifacts of other centuries still command'. They are, he says, 'dreams of a lost palace … a compulsion to regain some of the opulence of the past … a search for Baroque splendour'. Given the French taste for antiquity and the significant presence that busts and statues already enjoy in French homes, Oriel Harwood's sculptural interpretations of civilization's classics provide an up-to-date manner in which to continue a time-honoured tradition.

*Available from David Gill
Tel. 44 171 589 5946*

TOTEMIC

CHAIR

*Christian Astuguevieille's creations are concerned with the reintroduction of a tactile quality to design. His chairs, tables and other **objets**, wrapped in rope or cotton cord in a manner inspired by tribal art and artifacts, are a reflection of the search for the modern totem – an object of meaning in a contemporary society largely detached from inanimate objects. Even if the meaning is obscure, Astuguevieille's totemic designs communicate by touch and feel, adding a 'primal' aspect to his unique and instantly identifiable furniture.*

*Christian Astuguevieille's designs are represented by David Gill in London and are available from his own shop in the Galerie Vivienne in Paris
Tel. 33 1 42936032*

CARTON

ART

*Matthias & Natalie are the Dolce & Gabbana of cardboard. Working exclusively in this **pauvre** material, they are the **auteurs** of creations that include tableaux, sculptures and **objets**. Their creativity also extends to graphic design, including a new label design for Kanterbräu. Crazy, fun and irreverent, their work has a certain spirit which is difficult to pin down. Titles for each piece are chosen from dictionaries or telephone books and the works are often inscribed with ludicrous slogans such as 'if you have a headache, cut off your head'. Their work is best described by Barbara Stoeltie as 'pseudo-advertising art'.*

*Paris Musées Boutiques
Tel. 33 1 42741302 or 33 1 40265665*

"If I were to be the ruler of France,
I would want to make Paris not only the most beautiful city
in the world, that the world has ever known,
but the most beautiful city that could ever be."

Napoleon Bonaparte